SMART PEOPLE DON'T HAVE A BOSS

Eddie Rodwell

3P PUBLISHING

Smart People Don't Have A Boss

First published in 2016 in the UK

Set in Giovanni 12pt

3P Publishing Ltd
C E C, London Road
Corby
NN17 5EU

A catalogue number for this book is available from the British Library

ISBN 978-1-911559-02-3

Cover design: Jamie Rae

To my wonderful wife Maureen without whom I would be nothing.

To my two children Matthew and Claire. I am so proud of you both.

To my grandchildren Joshua, Jude and Maisie. You are awesome.

To the team at 3P Publishing Ltd who have been fantastic at motivating me to get this book out of my head and onto paper.

To every customer and distributor who has helped me and supported me to create a business which has grown beyond my wildest dreams.

And most of all I dedicate this book to you my dear reader. You have invested your hard-earned cash in a book by an unknown author hoping, I imagine, to gain some insight into escaping a mundane world and transforming it into a world of possibility.

I hope you find this book a worthy companion on your journey.

Contents

PART ONE My Story

INTRODUCTION

I feel that I should explain the title of this book – “Smart People Don't Have A Boss!” Firstly, please note that it doesn't say “Clever People Don't Have A Boss”. There are many clever people who *do* have a boss. In fact, that is usually why the Boss hires them – *because* they are clever. They have a skill or attribute which he is willing to buy.

In taking on a worker the boss is also taking on a lot of responsibility and risk. There are overheads to be paid. The employee needs training, supervision, good working conditions and so on. They will be entitled to sick pay and holiday pay which, from the boss's point of view, is pay for doing nothing. On top of this the boss's enterprise has to make a profit otherwise there is no point being in business.

The employee, therefore, has to create enough money for the boss to cover not only his wages, but also part of the overheads and part of the profits of the business. It stands to reason then, that the employee is getting paid less than the income he or she is producing.

Many employees probably realise that they are not being paid what they are actually worth. So why do they stay an employee? I really don't know but I guess part of the answer is that they don't want to be a Boss.

It is the premise of this book that "Smart" people realise that they are not being paid what they are actually worth and are prepared to do something about it. Please note that "Smart" people are not, by my definition, necessarily "Clever". They just want a life where they are in control of their destiny.

Imagine what life would be like if you were the boss of your own life. You would do work you really enjoyed doing. You would take extended holidays and time off when it suited you. You would have an inflation linked income source which continued to pay you whether you worked or not. You would throw away the alarm clock, get up and go to bed whenever you wanted. You would also have enough money to leave a legacy to your children or a favourite charity.

You wouldn't have any pension worries because you would retire on an income which continued to increase. Would you like a life like that or is it just a pipe dream? Well I am here to tell you that I have done it.

Am I "Clever"? I don't think so. But I do think that over the years I have learned how to be "Smart". In this book, I will tell you how I got to where I am now and how you can do it too. There is nothing left out. All the details are here.

Whether you are 18 or 80, an employee, retiree or out of work, a single mum or a hard-working dad there is something here for you.

All you need is a dream. The desire to have a better life. The willingness to take action and the determination to follow a simple plan until you succeed. Ready? Take my hand and let the adventure begin!

CWR Rodwell - My Dad

CHAPTER ONE

MY EARLY LIFE

My father was born in 1897, the year of Queen Victoria's Diamond Jubilee. He was in his fifties when he married my mother having lost his first wife to stomach cancer. I don't think that he ever got over her death and that probably accounts for the fact that my sister, Linda, is named after her and that he drank more than he should have.

He was a Victorian father. Heavy handed and never one to discuss things with a child. Children should be "seen and not heard". We learned to stay out of his way. However, he had his good side. He read to us. Classic books like *Uncle Tom's Cabin, The Children of the New Forest, Black Beauty* and *Ivanhoe.* He made us tea in the morning before we went to school and, when he was out of work, he took us there himself.

Money was always in short supply. Breakfast was a hit and miss affair. Sometimes porridge, sometimes stale bread with sugar, always tea. The house was cold. In the winter ice formed on the inside of the bedroom windows.

Children were bathed together and clothes were dried in front of the living room fire. Winters seemed harsher then and London was still subject to smog which sometimes made it difficult to breathe. When it was smoggy we walked to school with handkerchiefs over our mouths. They had turned yellow by the time we got there.

Unlike many children, I loved school dinners. A proper meal including a pudding and sometimes 'seconds' from a generous dinner lady.

My mother was half my dad's age. She had come from 'the back of beyond' in Southern Ireland during the war. She was working behind a bar when she met him. He was middle aged, still handsome and with a sad story to tell. She fell in love. They married and three children followed. She stayed with him for the sake of the children. As a teenager, I remember asking her "How do you know if you are in love?" She replied "There is no such thing as love except a mother's love for her children".

She was clever but not educated and with my father not being the ideal breadwinner she had little choice than to do any work she could find, often working in factories late into the night and doing cleaning jobs during the day. Generally, this meant leaving the children at home on their own, since my father would be out at the greyhound racing or the pub. We sometimes accompanied him to the racing at Wembley or White City which was an adventure. He wasn't a lucky gambler. We always started out in hope, but inevitably returned in silent depression and despair. Often we were made to feel that it was our fault.

One memorable Christmas there was nothing to eat in the house and we were excitedly waiting for my father to come home from work with his week's wages. He was very late. Eventually he turned up exceptionally drunk, staggered in the door and slid down to the floor unconscious. I can still see my poor mother going through his pockets in the hope that there was some money left.

Life wasn't all bad. In the summer holidays, we were packed off to relatives in Ireland. I know that my mother borrowed the money to pay our fare. It was an overnight journey by train and boat. We travelled on our own from a very young age. We were met by our grandfather and stayed with an aunt who lived in a village on the Kerry coast. We had to fetch water from a hydrant in the road and most houses didn't have electricity, but we loved it. Over the years both electricity and sewerage (meaning flushing toilets) arrived. By the time I was a teenager the village had gained a cinema and an outside dancing place: 'The platform'. It even gained a hotel which attracted visitors from as far away as Dublin.

Our aunt and her husband kept a pig in a pigsty attached to their bungalow. We arrived for our holiday a little early one year and guiltily watched the pig being loaded onto a van for the market. We then helped to clean the pigsty which was to be our home for the duration of the holiday.

My mother had another sister who was housekeeper for a priest and for a treat took me to Ireland one Easter holiday. She was not to be trusted with a 10-year-old child. She left me there with another relative and returned to England on her own. At first I was delighted but there was no way to get me back to England and the authorities decided that if I had to stay there then I had to go to school. In those days, all ages of children were taught by a single teacher in a very large classroom. Lessons were taught in Gaelic which, of course, I didn't understand. I was allowed the privilege of sitting next to a cousin who would translate for me. I learned to count in Irish, say some prayers and sing rebel songs. We walked the three miles to school carrying our books and a lunch of bread and jam and a bottle of milk. In hot weather the milk had little lumps of butter in it having been churned on the way.

Returning to England I eventually went to a grammar school in Ealing. I hated it. It probably won't come as a surprise to you that, given my upbringing, I was very shy. I was also quite small for my age. This resulted in more than my fair share of being bullied. Our English teacher was a thin man with a large birth mark on his face. He greeted us on our first day by saying that it was his ambition to have us all beaten at least once by the end of the first term. He carried out his threat. Corporal punishment was administered using a specially manufactured instrument made of reinforced leather. My misdemeanour which warranted this punishment was leaving out the full stop at the end of a sentence.

I won't bore you with other tales from this horrendous establishment. Suffice to say that I played truant, failed all my 'O' levels and had to re-sit them a year later. It is enough to know that there is an online survivors group for ex-pupils.

CHAPTER TWO

THE ESCAPE ROUTE

My father's job was in sales. When I was first aware of what he did he was selling exotic foods to delicatessens. Gentleman's relish and chocolate covered ants (really!) – that sort of thing. He didn't drive, so travelled by bus with a very heavy leather case full of samples.

One summer he collected flowers from the garden, wrapped them in fancy paper and sent us children out to sell them on the street. We approached gentlemen returning home from work hoping they would buy these bargain bunches. He waited at home for us to return with the loot like some latter-day Fagin.

I also made some money by selling soap and talcum powder door to door after school. I don't suppose that a child would be allowed to go door to door in the dark in London these days. At least it now seems like a dangerous thing to do. I tell you the above because sales and selling have been a big part of my life from a very young age.

I eventually got 4 'O' levels and started work in a laboratory. Despite my experiences at secondary school I loved learning, so enrolled at night school. Being treated as an adult I thrived. I got an ONC and at my second job was given day release to study for an HNC in sciences.

My first job entailed testing ingredients being used for making stomach powder in case they contained too much arsenic. Eventually I had absorbed so much arsenic myself that all the tests I did showed positive results and I had to be taken off that work.

In my next job, I worked in the x-ray spectrographic lab testing precious metals for impurities. It was here that I got my first introduction to a computer and started a lifelong fascination with computing. This machine was programmed with magnetic cards and made our analysis work a whole lot faster and easier.

It was also here that I had two life changing events. Firstly, I read *The Power Of Positive Thinking* by

Norman Vincent Peale which helped me to overcome my shyness and believe that with God's help I could do anything which I put my mind to.

The second event propelled me into the world of entrepreneurship. I had been working at the factory for nearly two years when I was called into the boss's office. He opened a drawer, took out a picture and asked me if I knew who that was. It was a picture of my boss in a Home Guard uniform. He was on duty outside the factory guarding it in case the Germans should parachute in! He was very proud of that picture but what went through my head was this thought 'He is one rung above me and has been in this job since the war!!' I was terrified that I could be trapped into doing the same thing. Entombed there for the next forty years. The following day I gave in my notice.

Not knowing what I was going to do but also knowing that I couldn't continue to live at home without any income, I quickly did an audit of my skills and aptitudes. These didn't amount to much. I had, however, learned to drive and had a fairly respectable car. There was an opportunity to go self-employed as a mini cab driver, so that's what I did.

I joined a firm in Acton, purchased an A-Z of London and I was off. With tips I made a decent living, but being self-employed working in someone else's business didn't feel that great. I was still being told what to do, how much to charge and when to turn up for a shift. In other words, it was just like being an employee without any of the benefits.

After six months, I had had enough and together with one of the other drivers decided to start my own firm. We found premises to rent under the railway arches in Du Cane Rd near Shepherd's Bush, got some cards printed and we were in business. We posted cards through the letter boxes around and about and never had to advertise after that. We took on drivers, I bought a car which could be used for weddings and my girlfriend, Maureen, and my dad, who was now retired, manned the phones.

We were just down the road from Wormwood Scrubs prison. If you watch any of the old black and white films you will recognise the iconic gates through which passed many of the greatest criminals of the day. These included the spy George Blake who escaped from the prison in 1966 by climbing over the perimeter wall using a ladder made of knitting needles. He eventually surfaced in Moscow and lived on a pension provided by the KGB. My contact was with inmates of a much more mundane variety. One of our contracts involved taking remand prisoners to court or perhaps convicts who were being transferred to another jail. These low risk villains sat in the back of my car handcuffed between two warders.

On one occasion as we were approaching a central London court one of these miscreants managed to escape from his cuffs, leapt from the car and ran at top speed up the street. He was hotly pursued by the officers shouting at the top of their voices "Stop that man!" An obliging gent stuck his foot out which sent the felon headlong to the ground. Passers-by held him down and as we caught up with him I heard him say "Thank gawd for the great British public".

Another time I was taking a chap who was out on bail to meet his girlfriend. He was sitting in the back, but she got in the front passenger seat and gave me directions for where she wanted to go. We set off down Shepherd's Bush High Street but seemingly this was the wrong direction for him. He leaned across the seat, grabbed me by the throat, yanked my head back and started to throttle me. The car was still moving, but I was no longer driving. The girlfriend's screams brought him to his senses and he let go just in time for me to regain control without smashing headlong into the approaching cars. We stopped long enough for everyone to calm down and set off again following his orders. I have never been so relieved as when they both exited my cab.

CHAPTER THREE

BACK TO WORKER DRONE

The business was going well so Maureen and I decided to get married. Our honeymoon was to be an organised bus tour lasting three months and going as far as Russia. This was all on a hippie style double-decker London bus. Russia was still firmly behind the Iron Curtain so this was going to be a great adventure.

Neither of our parents had any money so we had to pay for the wedding ourselves. At least we had our own wedding car. One of the mini cab drivers drove it for me and we had a beautiful day. Around 100 guests and 100 pounds behind the bar paid for drinks all day – those were the days! We were married in the local Catholic church and the ladies of the parish produced a wonderful wedding breakfast for very little money. In the evening we had use of the church hall complete with dancing to an Irish band.

Our wedding night was spent in a nearby hotel and the following day we set off for a few days in Cornwall. We planned to stay in bed-and-breakfast accommodation and, just in case we couldn't find anywhere, we had a tent in the boot.

That summer of 1973 was very hot indeed. The result being that bed- and-breakfast accommodation was scarce and we stayed in the tent for a week. Our return to London brought into sharp relief our lack of planning. We had nowhere to live. With all the excitement of wedding planning this small detail had passed us by. I asked my dad if we could stay at his house while we made other, more permanent, arrangements. He grumpily agreed. A few days later we had secured a one bed flat in Neasden and moved in to our first marital home.

Travelling to Russia but not having a proper home now seemed a reckless thing to do. So, we cancelled the trip and started looking for a house. There was nothing we could afford in London and we also ran into another snag. No one would give us a mortgage because I was self-employed. If we were ever to get a house of our own I needed a job.

Becoming a worker drone again wasn't very attractive but it had to be done. With my qualifications and background what do you think was the best job for me? I became a Betting Shop manager! Ladbrokes provided the training and I was, as they say, "off to the races". Any spare time was spent house hunting. We travelled further and further North up the M1 looking for something we could afford. Eventually we arrived at the steel town of Corby. Neither of us had ever heard of the place, but the houses were cheap.

One of the reasons behind the cheap housing was that Corby, at the time, was the murder capital of Europe. Luckily we didn't know that and so we bought our first house.

I stayed with Ladbroke Racing for five years. Moving from manager to relief manager and finally promotions co-ordinator. Technology was advancing and I got an early calculator. This battery-operated marvel had flashing LED lights and was a fantastic addition to running a betting office. Up to that point calculating the winnings was all done by working it out in your head or on paper. This was time consuming and prone to error. Using a calculator speeded things up tremendously. I even ran courses for other managers in using this new technology.

Corby had a very high number of people who had come from Scotland to work in the Steel Works when it was run by the Scottish Company – Stewarts and Lloyds. As a Promotions Co-ordinator, this gave me a big opportunity. We sponsored the "World Haggis Eating Contest". It was an annual event and we gave the media an angle by not only offering odds on the outcome, but by persuading one of the betting shop cashiers to take part. She was the event's first woman contestant! Of course, she wore a Ladbrokes sash and around the venue we had strategically placed banners with the company name emblazoned on them. It not only made the local paper but TV news bulletins on both ITV and BBC. Fantastic publicity for the company at a total cost of £50.

Running a betting shop was a very pressurised environment and staff didn't last very long. You will get some idea about this if I tell you that after five years I received a "long service" award.

CHAPTER FOUR

EDDIE IS MAGIC

In the previous chapters I have left out one very important detail which had a huge impact on my life because I feel that it deserves a chapter to itself.

My hobby, ever since I was a very young child, has been magic. It started when my father showed me the one trick he knew – How to vanish a penny. I don't know where he learned how to do it but years later I found out that he used a classic magician's method called "the French drop". I was hooked. My evenings were spent studying magic books from the library and I found that I was quite good at taking complicated instructions from the books and making them into magic which would fool people. For a small child with self-esteem issues this was magic indeed!

My aunt, the same one who left me behind in Ireland, gave me some pocket money and I was able to travel to the West End where there were various magic dealers and I also purchased magic props through the post.

In my teenage years, I spent most Saturdays at dealers and all the money I had on magic books and props. Most dealers had places in and around Soho. I would pass premises advertising all sorts of sexual delights to spend the day learning and talking about ways to do card tricks or make things disappear. On one of these visits I met the wonderful Tommy Cooper. He had just come back from a gig abroad and had the place in stiches just describing his problems with overweight luggage on the flight. He was a very big man with a huge personality and I could have listened to his stories for ever.

On another occasion, I was talking to a magician who had just returned from Buckingham Palace where he had been entertaining the royal children. He showed them a close-up trick which he had invented. I purchased the secret from him and it became a fixture in all my future performances. I have kept the method secret all my life. If we ever meet I hope that I get the chance to show it to you because it is still my favourite trick.

I joined a couple of magic clubs and took part in their competitions. I'm pleased to say that I won prizes for both close-up and stage magic and eventually I became a member of the Magic Circle in London. It is a bit of an ordeal to be accepted because you must do a performance for judges who, being very experienced magicians, know exactly how you are doing the tricks. All of this meant that I developed a nagging thought in my mind 'Could I do magic professionally?' Two things stopped me. Nobody in my family was in showbiz so I really didn't have any contacts and, more importantly, I was still chronically shy.

My breakthrough came when I saw an advert for a talent contest at a local Corby pub. My wife, Maureen, encouraged me to enter and I put together a short comedy magic act. The back of the small stage was covered in mirrors which isn't exactly ideal for a magician and there was a microphone which I had never used before. Despite all that I somehow won the heat. There were more heats which I also won and the pub organised a coach to take me and a pub full of supporters to the grand finale. I would love to be able to tell you that I won that too, but I didn't.

However, one of the judges asked me who my agent was. Of course, I didn't have an agent because I had never worked professionally. He said he was surprised and put me on his books. The very next weekend I was part of a show and, more importantly, getting paid.

I never had any desire to be famous. You must have superb talent and unbelievable drive to make it in show-business and I met acts who had been at the top but were now on the way down and they were all rather sad. I worked with comedians who had to down half a bottle of whiskey just to get the courage to go back on stage one more time. I also worked with acts who, in the dressing room, told stories about how great they were but subsequently went down so badly that I had to take them off stage.

I saw myself as a "jobbing" magician. I worked most weekends and nearly every day in December. My first gigs on Sundays were with strippers. In those days there was a tradition of pubs and clubs having three strippers and a comedian on Sunday afternoons. As you can imagine, the comedians had a hard time because the men had come to see the girls and so, to hold the audience, they tended to be very blue. If you think that the audience didn't have any interest in the comics then imagine how interested they were in a young, shy, non-swearing magician! Somehow I survived and I have to tell you that it is very unnerving sharing a dressing room with strippers when you are a shy Catholic boy! They were all nice women though and mostly just doing it to support themselves and their children. When I met them in the street with their family they would say hello and I could genuinely say "I nearly didn't recognise you with your clothes on!"

I have always had an interest in hypnotism and I thought that it would make a great finish to my comedy magic act if I pretended that I was going to hypnotise people. I would get the audience to stand and press their hands together tightly then separate their hands about six inches and once again press them together even more tightly. I got them to speed up this apart and together movement until they found themselves clapping whereupon I said "Thank you for the standing ovation and goodnight!!" It got a laugh and more importantly allowed the agent to sell me by saying "He always gets a standing ovation at the end of his act."

One evening a young man came backstage and asked if I could really hypnotise people. He wanted me to help his sister who had an eating disorder. Of course, I couldn't help but he was so sincere and so desperate that it made me want to investigate hypnotism further. I found a course on stage hypnosis and really wanted to try it. Now with a magic act you can practice in front of a mirror, but with hypnosis you need lots of other people. The only way is to go in front of an audience and do it, even though you have never done it before and really have no idea if it will work. Luckily for me it did.

At the time, there were very few hypnotists on the circuit and it had never been on television so it was always new to the audience. It was scary but I loved it and a big side benefit was that it paid better than being a magician. I also took courses in therapeutic hypnosis, NLP and counselling which meant that I could help people like that young man's sister.

Eventually I got two more agents who gave me work all over the country mostly working army camps and entertaining the squaddies. They are a tough crowd for most ordinary acts but great for a hypnotist because they are not afraid to volunteer for something which average people find quite scary and threatening.

I worked abroad too. In Germany entertaining the troops and for Thompsons in Ibiza, Majorca and Minorca entertaining the holiday makers.

I could probably fill another book with stories of those days, but it is time to return to the world of sales.

CHAPTER FIVE

FLYING FROM SUCCESS TO FAILURE

Whilst the magic and hypnotism provided a reasonable income, you only get paid when you work and entertainment can be hit and miss. Some months you can have a lot of shows and others almost none. For some reason I have never been able to fathom, as soon as I had a booking for one particular night, two or three bookings would come in all wanting me for the same night.

One good thing is that it is evening work so you can still have a day job. I left Ladbroke Racing and returned to my first love – selling. Specifically, selling insurance. Selling insurance is a tough business because it is an intangible product which no one really wants. I wasn't great at it. Maybe I lacked the salesman's killer instinct to "go for the close". However, I did OK at it. So much so that I won a cruise around the Greek Islands with my wife for the number of sales I had made.

This was an amazing outcome. Having very little money, no steady income and two small children, here we were off on our first cruise. I am forever grateful to friends from church who said that they would look after the children while we went away. It was the first time I had been in an aeroplane. As a small child, I remember looking at an aeroplane flying overhead and thinking "I never want to go in one of those". To say I was scared of flying would be to put it mildly. No amount of alcohol made it any better. In later years when I was gigging in the Balearics I had to fly between the islands every week but I never enjoyed it. I could have used self-hypnosis to cure myself but chose not to do so. Something psychological there Mr Freud!

Selling insurance can qualify you for many prizes. The insurance companies want to encourage sales and these incentives can be quite rewarding. In one instance, I sold the largest policy that the company had ever sold. The commission was a year's salary for most people and they also gave my wife and I a holiday in Jamaica. More flying, but this time we went first class. More leg room and glasses of champagne seemed to help my flying phobia a bit!

I felt that the next step for me was to start my own business once again rather than just be a self-employed sales person. I saw an opportunity to buy a franchise in a financial planning business. It was with an American parent company who had sold a master franchise to a Brokerage in Scotland. It was very advanced for its time. There were pre-organised seminars, some bespoke products and agencies with all the major insurance and investment companies. There was also a computerised financial planning program. In other words, it was right up my street. One small snag was the considerable amount of money needed to buy the franchise. Luckily NatWest bank obliged with a loan. I went to Edinburgh for a week's training, we took a 20-year lease on offices in Kettering and all seemed rosy.

For a while it was. We had lots of training, including Maureen spending three months at the Franchise Headquarters in Miami. This left me to run the business at home and look after two little children but we felt it was worth it. We had quarterly training meetings with the other franchisees in nice locations like Gleneagles in Scotland. I even got a free trip to Miami myself. The company flew me out to give a talk and put me up in the Fontainebleau Hilton where you can have breakfast on the beach and Pina-colada made with coconuts freshly cut from the tree.

Things at home took a turn for the worse. The master franchisee became ill and had to give up work. He had been like the captain of the ship guiding the business, translating the American sales processes into ways which suited the British temperament and being immensely supportive to the franchisees. He was a man with huge experience and was a great loss.

When a ship has no captain, it can quickly run aground and that is exactly what happened. We were all struggling when a new master franchisee bought the business and we all breathed a sigh of relief.

The new owners were two brothers from Northern Ireland. There was a re-launch in a top hotel and were back on an even keel. A few months later our monthly commissions were not paid. There had been a computer error and we had to wait until the following month. That month came and still no money. Finally, the penny dropped when, in the third month there was still no money and the brothers had disappeared never to be seen again.

You obviously can't run a business without any money and franchisees began to panic. The Americans organised a meeting in Central London where they told us that they didn't have any legal responsibility for us since our contract was with the Northern Ireland Master Franchisees. However, they did feel that they had some moral responsibility and would put in a manager to oversee things here – provided that we all stumped up some more cash. Being experienced business people in the financial planning sector you would think we would have smelled a rat, wouldn't you? But we didn't and all the franchisees coughed up many more thousands of pounds.

Financial services were going through a regulatory upheaval at the time and to remain independent advisors, which was key to our role, we all had to jump through hoops. Lots of forms to fill and exams to complete. None of which made us any money and took a lot of time. All of this was organised by the new manager, a larger than life South African who had swanky offices in the world trade centre in London.

D-day came. The day when financial advisors had to be fully compliant with the new rules and fully independent or become tied agents working with a single insurer. We were called to a meeting at the Head Office to get our new fully compliant credentials. It was not to be. The South African told us that we were not going to be independent after all and he had arranged a tie to a major insurer. We were dumfounded.

The business couldn't possibly work that way and it collapsed. Some franchisees lost their homes and we found ourselves with no income and huge debts. The bank called in our loan. It was a desperate time. We had no money coming in apart from the entertainment and we thought that we would never be solvent again. Maureen said that she was going to write a cookery book called "101 recipes for living on lentils!"

Not wishing to be beaten we formed a company with two other ex-franchisees and went into the general insurance business. We also started to sell Health Insurance. This is a very niche market which most brokers avoid because it can be technically difficult and is mainly sold to the business rather than the domestic community.

We were working from home having managed to get rid of the lease and Maureen hit the phone making appointments for me to see business people within a 50-mile radius of Corby. Phone calls at the time were expensive and all that phoning meant that we had a huge bill.

I saw an article in the local paper which said that a new company had a little box which you could plug into your phone line. It routed the calls away from BT to cheaper carriers and thus reduced your phone bill. It sounded ideal for people like me. Google didn't exist back then and the paper only gave a name but no contact details. I can't tell you how I found the company but I did. They sent me details and also said that they were looking for representatives. It seemed like a good way to increase my income so I joined. If I only made £25 extra a month it would pay for a new computer which I desperately needed. Little did I know that it was a decision which would change our lives for ever.

PART TWO Your Road To Success

Do you have the courage
to bring forth the treasures
that are hidden within you?
Jack Gilbert
www.smartpeoplebook.co.uk

CHAPTER SIX

WHY ARE YOU HERE?

We will come back to my life story later but now let's talk about you. How old are you? Are you happy with your life so far? Do you have dreams you haven't yet achieved. Or have you given up on your dreams? Do you want to continue doing what you are doing now for the rest of your life?

Are you young but don't have a job?

Do you have a job which you find boring and unsatisfying?

Are you a single mum or dad finding it hard to make ends meet?

Perhaps you have a job you enjoy but you will retire on very little money.

For many people retirement is a struggle either because they have little money or because they feel bored and, more usually, both of those things.

Maybe you have a business of your own like me but are struggling to make it work and provide a decent living.

Do you feel fulfilled? Is every day a joy and full of promise? I wish that I could sit down with you over a cup of coffee and hear your answers.

Sadly, many people are living lives which are unfulfilled and almost desperate. They party away the weekend because they are dreading going back to work on Monday. They are looking forward to a retirement where they will have to live on an income which is about a third of what they have to live on now.

In a nutshell, they are living but don't have a life. I wonder if you can relate?

If any of the above applies to you then I have some wonderful news for you. This book which you bought, borrowed or stole (it's OK I don't want to know) has the power to change your life for the better.

And if you don't have any of the problems above, it will reveal to you a way in which you can help those less fortunate to have a fantastic life.

It is not going to be easy – you are going to have to work – but I have faith in you. You can do it and it will be worth it for you, your family and the wider community.

So, what are your options?

If you are going to escape from a world where you have a boss who decides how much you are going to get paid, what you are going to do, when to get up and when you are allowed to go on holiday. If you are looking forward to relative poverty in retirement or are already retired and not only poor but terminally bored.

I think that you have three realistic options – four if you count doing nothing!

1. Start a business of your own.
2. Buy a franchise.
3. Join a referral marketing company.

Let's look at option one.

Do you have a skill or hobby which you can turn into a money-making venture? Maybe you have an invention which you can manufacture and promote. Alternatively, you could start small as a window cleaner say or cleaning cars. You could open a shop or tea-room; the possibilities are endless. Just look around any high street or the small ads in the newspaper and you will get lots of ideas.

So why don't many people go down this route? There are several reasons. First you must have an idea and people in general are not good at coming up with ideas.

Secondly you need a business plan and, if you have never done it before, that is quite difficult.

Thirdly, you will need money and possibly lots of it.

Finally, it is risky. Most new businesses fail. Which is why many people go for ....

Option Two – A Franchise

A Franchise has a proven business model so it is less likely to fail. Although, having read my story, you will understand that failure is still a possibility.

Many people have found fame and fortune with a franchise. The downside is that you need a lot of money to start a franchised business.

The most famous burger franchise is likely to cost you over half a million pounds. And whilst there are many franchises which cost far less it can be a costly option. If you decide to go down this route, I have a few tips for you.

- Go to the Franchise Exhibition. Get all the information you can about franchises which interest you but commit to nothing on the day.
- Pick a franchise in an industry which excites you. Don't just choose the one which appears to have the most profit potential.
- Visit existing franchises. Not just the "star" ones introduced to you by the master franchise holder but ones which you have found through your own research.
- Visit their premises, introduce yourself as a potential franchisee and offer to buy the owner a coffee or lunch in return for his or her honest opinion.
- You want to find out the total cost not just the upfront fee. How much support and training is provided? What day to day life is like running the franchise?
- Preferably take a trusted friend with you. Someone who has their own business already would be ideal.

Whilst buying a franchise is a much safer option than starting your own business from scratch, the amount of money required is a big barrier for most people. So, let us take a look at ....

Option Three – A Referral Marketing Company

Fair warning: I am biased here because this is the route I have chosen. Remember the company I found that reduced the cost of phone calls by using a smart little box to route the calls away from British Telecom?

It turned out to use the referral marketing business model. Rather like franchising in the early years, referral marketing or network marketing had a bad reputation when it first started. There were disreputable companies who sold almost worthless products and sucked people in to all sorts of "get rich quick" schemes.

Government regulation and the entry of household name companies has ended all that. It is now a multi-million-pound worldwide industry with a turnover bigger than the film and music industries combined.

So why have so many companies adopted this business model and why are so many ordinary people involved?

From a company point of view, it uses the most effective advertising model ever invented – word of mouth. For the distributor representative, it has all the benefits of a franchise: It is your own business and you have a proven business model, training and support with a low cost of start-up. In the UK that is a maximum of £200.

There are over a hundred companies using this business model in the UK and thousands worldwide. So, you have plenty of choice and very little financial risk. Part three of this book is devoted to the nuts and bolts of running a successful network marketing business. It includes lots of hints, tips and ideas which I have learned over the eighteen years I have been involved in the industry but before we get down to the "nitty gritty" I want to address something I feel very passionate about – "Work – Life Balance".

CHAPTER SEVEN

GOING THROUGH LIFE WITH A WONKY WHEEL

On my desk at home there is a statue which I picked up on a trip to America. It is of a large cat in a house coat, smoking a fat cigar. Underneath the legend reads "I don't want to be a millionaire – I just want to live like one!"

That just about sums up my philosophy of life. Being an actual millionaire carries a lot of worry and responsibility with it I would imagine. You would be worried about losing your fortune, personal security would most likely be a problem and it would be difficult to know who your real friends were.

On the other hand, being a millionaire would give

you lots of choices and freedom to do what you want to do.

Few millionaires have a boss. So being your own boss is one step towards having the millionaire lifestyle, however, many people have found that single minded focus on a business goal is very unhealthy. They are not happy and the pressure can lead to mental problems, an early heart attack and the breakup of relationships. The trick is to have a balanced life!

There are six main areas in life to focus on and business is only one of them. Too much emphasis on any one area will mean that you have a "wonky wheel" and your passage through life will not be as smooth as it could be.

THE BALANCED LIFE EXERCISE:

This exercise is best carried out with your "significant other" if you have one. Choose a time when you have no other distractions and give yourself a score out of ten for each of these areas of your life. Where ten means that you are really happy, successful and fulfilled and one means that you are unhappy, unfulfilled, and unsuccessful or perhaps there is nothing happening in that area of your life at all.

- Work or Business
- Spiritual / Religious

- Sport / Recreation
- Family / Relationships
- Healthy Lifestyle
- Self-development / Education

There are no right or wrong answers here, only your own subjective judgement but I know from experience that when you are in a situation it is sometimes hard to be objective. That is why it is really good to do this exercise with a partner.

If you are struggling, then take a look at how much time you spend on each area. For instance, if you spend 150 hours a week at work and only 30 minutes on exercise that is obviously not healthy!

For those of you who are a stay at home mum or dad that is your job. It is probably the most important job in our society, but if you do it more than full-time, meaning that you don't get a break or go out with friends once in a while, it will eventually become a chore which can lead to unhappiness for both you and the children. Even here, where you are doing a key job, balance is important.

What about self-development? If you are going to be your own boss, you will have to learn new skills. If you are going to be really successful, you are going to have to become a new person! Do you think that last statement is an exaggeration? It isn't.

To run your own business requires skills which you almost certainly don't possess. One of the key skills is maintaining a positive outlook in the face of adversity. To take a line from an old song – "There may be trouble ahead". In fact, there *will* be trouble ahead. How you deal with it will determine your long-term success or failure.

What kind of trouble? Everything life can throw at you. Sometimes it will feel as though anything and everything is going wrong. People will let you down. Technology will fail. The economy will change. Your health will take a dip. And all of these things may happen at once. How are you going to cope?

Self-development is the answer and it has to be a permanent part of your life as an entrepreneur. Reading is essential. At least half an hour a day. Perhaps the best time to do that reading is in the morning. If you can't manage that, then 10 minutes in the morning, 10 at lunch time and 10 minutes before you go to bed. Or get yourself an iPod or the equivalent and listen to a book as you exercise or do the housework.

If you are not doing that already, please start today. If you take nothing else from this book, please start today. You will become a new creature, a different person and be well on your way to success.

I would start by reading *The Power of Positive Thinking* by Norman Vincent Peale. It is the book which launched today's thriving personal development genre. Next I would read anything by Jim Rohn. Look him up on YouTube and you can listen to his best speeches for free. You will also need to read books which are relevant to the venture you undertake.

Whilst you can "wing it" in business for a while, you will never get to the top without education. That education is freely available in books, audios and videos. When you have the cash, you will want to take courses to speed up your progress and increase your knowledge. I hated school, but I learned to love learning. You will have to adopt that attitude as well.

Let us return to the exercise.

If you have equal numbers in each area congratulations, you have a balanced life. However, if one or two areas have higher numbers than all the others, you have an unbalanced life and are travelling along with a "wonky wheel". That is likely to be uncomfortable and you are in danger of falling off – with ill health, broken relationships and financial difficulties the possible outcome.

Are you surprised by the result of this little exercise? Have you gained a clearer insight into what is going well and what are the possible reasons for any problems you may be having?

Relax – most people need to make adjustments. The next thing to do is to create a plan of action. Look at each area. Let us assume that you have a 9 in the work category, but 6 in every other area. That is actually quite good although you can see that your life is not balanced.

The question now is – How can you get each of the "six" areas up to "nine"?

This goal setting should also be done with your partner, if you have one. Maybe you need to exercise more. Maybe you need to start reading motivational literature. Maybe you need to adopt a healthier eating regime or spend more time with your family.

Whatever you need to do, it is likely to take time. For me that meant getting up an hour earlier each day. It is surprising how quickly you can get used to doing so.

Like most things having a balanced life is simple even though it is not easy. It requires work but is supremely worth it.

If you need help, take a look at the bibliography for an excellent book on the subject. There are also suggestions for books you can read which will help you in each area of life as you aim for balance.

Area of Life	Score
Work / Business	
Spiritual / Religious	
Sport / Recreation	
Family/ Relationships	
Healthy Lifestyle	
Self-Development/ Education	

In the next chapter, we are going to look at the biggest reason that people fail or never get started: worry.

CHAPTER EIGHT

WORRY

Of all the human emotions **worry** can be the most debilitating and it is also the most useless. The dictionary definition of worry is "to think about problems or unpleasant things that might happen in a way that makes you feel unhappy and frightened".

Worrying is a passive activity. Unfortunately, it seems to be built into our nature and some people have turned it into an art form. "He (or she) is a born worrier" is commonly heard about certain people.

If you have never started a business of your own, worry is almost certainly the thing that stopped you in the past and may be stopping you now. Worry that you will fail. Worry that it will cost too much.

Worry about having the necessary skills. Worry about what your friends will say. Worry about what the boss will say. The list of worries is almost endless.

Unless you overcome your worries your dream stops here. Let me help you.

The first thing to realise is that worry is totally natural. However, it is all happening in your head so the best thing to do is to get it onto paper.

Yes, write out your worry!

Look at what you have written.

I am willing to bet that when you see it written down it will have already lost some of its power over you.

Now ask yourself this question. "Is there something practical that I can do about this worry?" If there is, then go ahead and do it.

If there is nothing you can do about it, you have my permission to worry about it for 10 minutes. If you believe in the power of prayer (I do) ask God to help you then pop the paper in your "Worry jar" and get on with your day. Don't look at what you have written for the rest of the month. At the end of the month you can empty the jar and look at your worries. Most will not have happened. Some you will have acted on and made them better. For the very, very few that came to pass there was nothing practical you could have done anyway and with God's help you will have got through them.

Over time you will find yourself worrying less. You may even turn the corner and start to laugh about things that used to worry you. I am indebted to Norman Vincent Peale for this technique. Norman was a chronic worrier, but became one of the most famous authors of his age.

If "What will people say" is one of your worries about starting a business of your own, or worse still, your friends are critical once you have started (which is quite common) let us confront that worry together.

"Misery loves company" and your friends and family are all in their comfort zone getting on with their lives. Have you seen one of those mobiles which are often hung over baby's cots to keep the child amused? They consist of several hanger shapes which have small items at each end and are suspended from a central cord. They are delicately in balance and gently move around in the breeze. If you were to remove one of the items at the end of one of the rods the whole assembly would tip.

That is a very good analogy for your friends and relatives and the relationships between you. You all have your acknowledged place and everyone knows where they fit in, but if you do something unexpected and, possibly out of character, the whole assembly tips.

People start to feel out of balance. You have challenged the *status quo*. Some will try to drag you back in order that the system is in balance again. You have made them feel uncomfortable and the quickest way that they can get comfortable again is to stop you doing whatever you are doing.

This lack of support for your new business and sometimes even open hostility is masked as "concern for your welfare". It comes as a shock to new entrepreneurs and is often enough for them to abandon the enterprise and scuttle back to safety. "It didn't work for me" they will say and their now comfortable and supportive friends will sympathise, put a real or figurative arm around them and give them a hug. I have seen it happen numerous times and it is horrible to watch.

It is probably the main reason for failure amongst people who attempt to start a business like mine. So, it is important that you are prepared and know what to do.

1) The lack of support, worry and concern for your welfare by those nearest and dearest to

you is not real. Although it may feel real to them it is actually a defence mechanism protecting their own egos.

2) Those people do not pay your mortgage.
3) Those people will not be paying your pension when you retire.
4) The only person responsible for the outcome of your life is you.
5) It is time to make a stand. You have decided to take control of your life so don't let others knock you off track.
6) Have an explanation ready for why you have taken this new path. "I want to have an extra income so that I can give my children the life they deserve" or "I was going to retire in poverty and decided to do something about it before it was too late" will go a long way towards calming things down. Understanding why you are doing what you are doing is often all it takes to turn around someone who is being unsupportive.
7) Eventually, and it may take a long time, the system will come back into balance and people will say "I always knew you would be successful" – just smile and thank them.
8) If you are looking for people to join you in your enterprise these new converts can be some of your best prospects. It may have

taken them many years to come around to your way of thinking but now you can help them to break free too.

By now I hope that you have decided to start a business of your own in the referral marketing industry and not to let anything stand in your way.

Congratulations! It is time to begin. Let's start by looking at how to choose a referral marketing company that will be right for you.

You will see companies referred to as "Network Marketing Companies", "Referral Marketing Companies" and "Multi-Level-Marketing Companies (shortened to "MLMs"). They all mean the same thing and some are definitely better than others. Let me guide you along the path to a sensible choice in the next chapter.

CHAPTER NINE

CHOOSING A NETWORK MARKETING COMPANY

Broadly speaking there are two sorts of companies. Those that offer products and those that offer services.

The usual reason that companies choose to go down the network marketing route is that they have a product or service which requires explanation. Traditional advertising is quite effective if you have a "Me too" product which everyone understands but if your product is innovative and requires potential customers to be educated in the benefits, it would be very expensive to use the traditional route.

The vast majority of people like to stay with products and services they are familiar with and understand. Even if they are not ecstatic about them they will stay with "The devil they know" rather than risk trying something new.

However, if something is recommended by a friend who is already using the product they are more likely to try it. Therefore, the company is willing to pay you for introductions to your friends and acquaintances. They will now have access to potential customers via relationships which you have built up over many years. You will also explain the benefits enthusiastically because you are already a happy customer yourself.

Everybody wins. The company has a route to market which is cost effective. The customer gets the benefit of a product or service which enhances their life and you earn an extra income which can change your financial future for ever.

But which is the right company for you? Here are the main points you should consider before investing your time and money.

1) Does the company have a business which is going to last long into the future? You are going to need the company to survive long-term in order to pay out your residual income in retirement. Many businesses fail because of poor management so check out who is running the company, how long they have

been in business and how much experience they have.

2) Does it have a product or service which will be bought by the general public and on a repeat basis. If the bulk of sales is created by distributors buying the product themselves then you should avoid the company.
3) Is the commission plan realistic and fair? Will it genuinely produce "walk away" income? This is a really key point: make sure that you understand what you have to do in order to get paid. Talk to existing people who are already involved and get them to explain the compensation plan. Ask them how it is working out for them.
4) Is there comprehensive training provided? Does the company itself provide training or is it all provided by the distributors? My own company spends millions of pounds on training distributors but this is quite unusual. So, if the training is mainly provided by the distributors themselves, you need to join a successful and supportive team.

   These are all questions you should get answered ***before*** you join the company.
5) Perhaps the two most important questions to ask yourself are:

a) "Would I buy this product or service if I wasn't getting paid to promote it?"
b) "Do I really love it, so that I can promote it with excitement and enthusiasm?"

The answer to those questions will, to a large extent, determine whether you just struggle along or ultimately break through to massive entrepreneurial success!

PART THREE

The Secrets Of Running A Successful Business

THE SUCCESS FLOWCHART

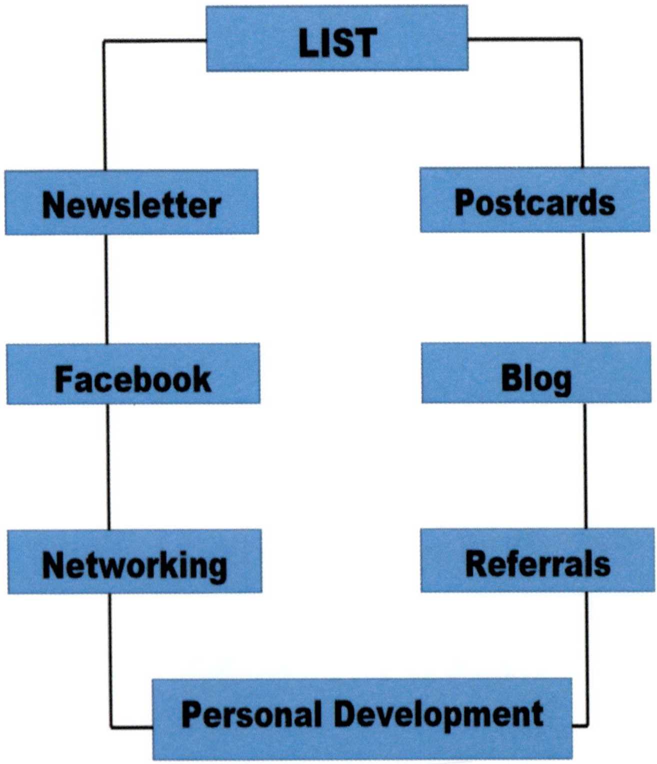

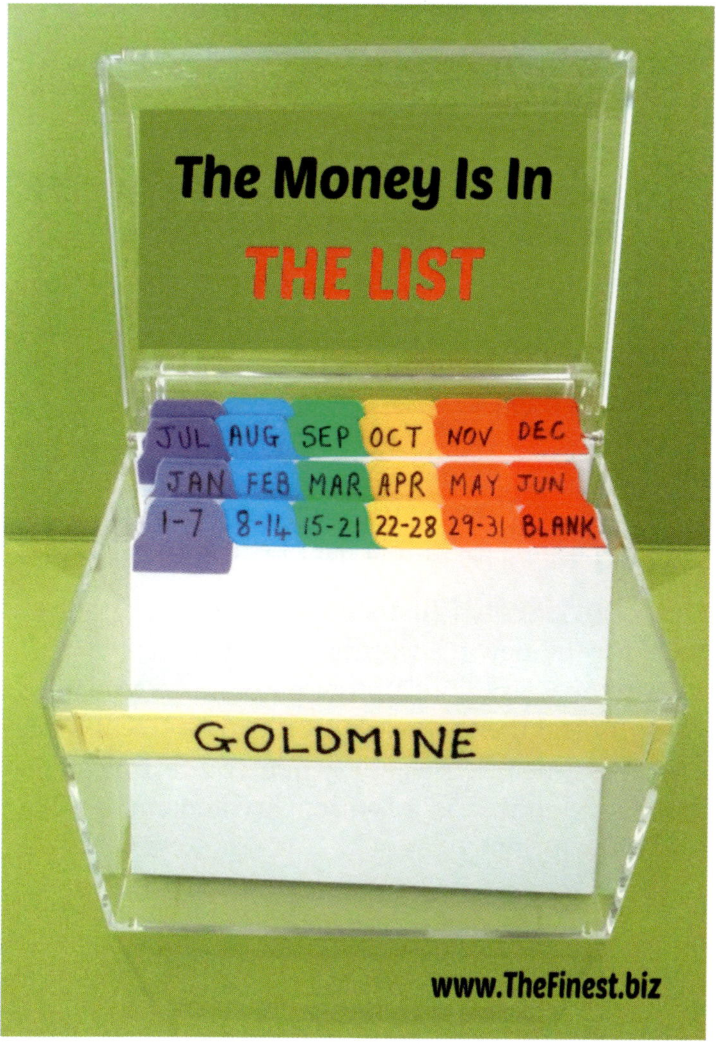
The Money Is In
THE LIST
JUL AUG SEP OCT NOV DEC
JAN FEB MAR APR MAY JUN
1-7 8-14 15-21 22-28 29-31 BLANK
GOLDMINE
www.TheFinest.biz

CHAPTER TEN

LIST BUILDING

In a network marketing company, you will, by definition, be marketing to your network. The starting point is to build a list of people you know.

This is an essential first step and too important to leave for the new distributor to do on their own. If you are new, ask your upline partner or sponsor to help you and then schedule a time to do it with your own team members as and when you recruit them. Make sure that it is a written list and not just in electronic format.

SOURCES:

Mobile phone

Social media

Christmas card list

Birthday card list

Wedding list

Club database

Internal work phone list

Memory jogger (usually supplied by your company)

Reassure the new distributor that they are not going to be asked to contact everyone on the list, only those that they feel comfortable contacting.

NEXT TASK – PRIORITISE THE LIST

1) Who do you know who would help you by becoming a customer?

2) Who do you know who is always looking for ways to make extra money?

3) Who on your list runs their own business?

4) Who on your list is over 50 and may not have a great pension sorted out?

5) Who is already retired and might be struggling financially?

6) Who belongs to a group or association? (Football club, social club, networking group, choir,

neighbourhood watch, Rotary, Round Table, PTA, church, golf club or darts club)

7) Who has a job where they work with lots of people?

8) Who has a job that they don't enjoy?

9) Who has a question related to your product or service?

10) Has another question related to your product or service.

What do I mean by a question related to your product or service? I mean a limiting factor created by the product or service you are going to promote. For example, if it is a slimming product "Is the person overweight?" If it is a product which helps people who are retired, then "Are they retired?" If you must own your own house to benefit, then "Do they own their own house?"

I'm sure that you understand and can come up with questions of your own. Even if the answer is "no" to the question or you don't know if it is "yes" or "no", you will still speak to these people. They may become distributors or they may introduce you to potential customers and distributors that are acquaintances of theirs. You will not contact them first however, because you have limited time and it makes sense to prioritise your activity.

Go through the list and place a tick against people in response to each question. We are going to start contacting the people who have the most ticks against their names.

According to a 2016 survey, the average Facebook user has over 150 "friends". Add to that all the people who are probably not Facebook friends like your doctor, the window cleaner, colleagues at work and old friends from school or people you have a business relationship with, like your car repairer or hair stylist and you can easily see how the average person can create a list of 200 people or more.

Assuming that each of those 200 has a network of their own amounting to 200 people then you have access to 200 x 200 = 40,000 people; either because you know them directly or you can be introduced to them by someone you already know.

It will depend on your compensation plan as to how many of those people you will need to enrol either as customers or distributors in order to be successful but it will certainly be a very small percentage.

The main stumbling block is not that people do not know enough people in order to be successful but that they do not do the basics properly. I cannot emphasise enough that **'the number one activity for a new distributor is to build a list'**.

Occasionally you will meet people who want to join your business but who say that they don't want to approach people they already know and so don't want to create a list. They want to work with people they don't already know – what is known in sales circles as "The cold market". I would say that network marketing is not a suitable occupation for these people. They will struggle and you will waste a lot of time with them. I'm sure that someone reading this book will be able to point to a person who is an exception to this rule, so if you want to sponsor them feel free. Just don't send them to me!

List building is not a "one off" activity. We should be adding to our list all the time. That is one good reason to have a written list. You can keep it in a notebook and take the notebook with you wherever you go.

Your list of customers, distributors and potential candidates is the most valuable business asset you possess, so make sure that you have copies.

A book, a card index and an electronic copy on your computer and "in the cloud" is not overkill. It is essential. If you lose your list, you will be out of business until you can create a new one and you may never recover all the data.

If you were opening a retail shop you would need stock and the names on our list are the stock for our network marketing business. Some of that stock will be “used up”. Either because they become customers or distributors or because they are not interested in being involved in either capacity.

So, our work boils down to 'making a list', 'adding to the list consistently' and then mining that list for the gold it contains.

Questions are the tools we use to mine the gold. Questions allow us to form the relationships which give us the right to add people to the list in the first place.

We all know how to do this. It isn't a 'technique'.

“Hello, how are you?"

"Is this your first networking event?"

"How do you know the bride and groom?"

"Have you been on holiday here before?"

We meet strangers. We create a relationship by asking open questions. We decide if we want to continue the relationship and, if we do, we add them to the list. We then continue the relationship by listening more than speaking until such time as it is appropriate to approach them about our business. That may be in 5 minutes or 5 years, depending on what we learn about them. This is the part which needs some skill. Up until this point anyone could do what is required, now a lot depends on our personal development.

We need listening skills, we need to know how to build rapport and our level of success will depend on how much the person "knows us, likes us and trusts us".

My best advice to you is – "Don't be a network marketing bore" and don't pounce on people the minute you spot that your business might be suitable for them. Have some respect for yourself and for them. Take your time. We have the most fantastic business and it can transform people's lives.

If you had a great big sack of precious jewels you might just let your new acquaintance peek inside the top of the sack. You wouldn't suddenly empty the sack of jewels on top of her! Instead of being impressed, it would probably kill her. Treat your precious jewel of a business in the same way and you won't go too far wrong.

RAY'S STORY

In June 2011 I became a customer of one of my friends who, a year earlier, had started a part-time business working from home. At that time, I didn't know anything about network marketing or that it was, in fact, a network marketing business he was running.

I was working full-time as a head teacher and my wife was also fully occupied as an occupational therapist. I loved my job but the stress was starting to take its toll and it was becoming less and less enjoyable.

Eventually I found myself in the doctor's surgery and he delivered his diagnosis. I was "burnt out" and if I continued doing what I was doing I wouldn't see 60! The only alternative seemed to be early retirement but that was a financial impossibility.

In May 2012, we took a short break in the Lake District with my friend and his wife and we started to talk about jobs, the doctor's diagnosis and my financial predicament. He suggested that I take a look at his business because it might fit in with my busy schedule and create the extra income needed to retire early.

I went to a business presentation and decided to join. I am now fully retired from teaching and the stress has completely vanished. I have qualified for a new car and, since I was already a happy customer myself, I have found no difficulty in promoting the services to others.

To top up my teacher's pension I have a regular monthly income which increases month by month. I meet lots of new and interesting people - who are mainly not teachers - and my wife plans on retiring at the end of the year as well.

That way we will both have our freedom back and can do what we want to do, when we want do it and go wherever the mood takes us.

I have goals and dreams for my future in the business but whether they occur quickly or slowly is irrelevant compared to the fact that I have my life back. And yes, I have every intention of enjoying my 60th birthday!

CHAPTER ELEVEN

LAUNCHING YOUR BUSINESS

"People don't have a prospecting problem

– they have an approach problem" - Anonymous

If you are new to being in business, there is an instant problem: "How do I approach my friends and acquaintances?" It often brings out a cold sweat in even the most confident of new entrepreneurs.

For some reason, we can invite people to a party but we can't invite them to look at our products, service or business opportunity. Despite what your sponsor or company may tell you there is a good reason for this fear. It is deep rooted and goes back to our caveman ancestry.

We relied on our family, or tribe, for protection and support. It was, quite literally, a matter of life or death. If we fell out with our friends we were easy prey for the next lion, tiger or enemy that came along.

In today's digitally connected world that translates as "not wanting to look a fool", "not wanting to take advantage of our friends" and "fear of failure". On top of that, our nearest and dearest might not be as supportive as we would want because we have "rocked the boat" and made them feel uncomfortable.

When starting out we lack credibility and that can be a huge handicap too. If we have started our new venture because we need to earn extra money, then we are clearly not as financially successful as we want to be. In that situation, it is difficult to approach people and convince them that we have found a way to earn lots of money.

Our chosen product or service can be a handicap too. What experience do we have in that particular field? How do we even know that what we are promoting is really good? It is no wonder that many people fail to get their business off the ground.

Yet, in reality, there are simple solutions to all these problems. With hard work and a sensible plan, we can not only survive the lions and tigers in our mind but eventually defeat them for good.

Firstly, do every bit of training that is available to you. You are potentially going to be earning more than a well-qualified doctor so it is foolish to imagine that you can do so without training.

Start on your personal development programme by reading appropriate books or listening to them on audio. There is a suggested list at the back of this book.

A key to surviving these early weeks is to realise that no one customer or distributor is going to make you rich. Your job isn't to sell them on your products, services or business but to find out if they are interested. Do not become attached to their answer because it is irrelevant. Some will be interested now, some later and some never. You just need to know which is which.

You have made your list and prioritised it. My mother would have bought whatever I was selling just to help me and it is highly likely that you will have one or two people like that on your list too. Now it is time to approach those people and the people with the most ticks against them with a simple request.

Your approach should be along these lines – "Hi mum, I've started a new business so that I can afford to take the children on holiday next year." (Make sure that you include your 'reason why'). "I'm feeling really nervous so would you do me a favour and take a look at what I have to offer. If you like it, you might want to become a customer but if not that is OK as I just need to practice my presentation."

That approach will work and remember what I said about not being attached to the outcome. If they become a customer or distributor that is fantastic but if not don't worry. You still have 39,999 people left!

Whilst we are getting some practice and approaching the "easy" people on our list we are also going to start "softening up" the rest of our list so that they are easy to approach too.

I call this the "Goldmine 200" process. Your list of 200 people is your Goldmine and you need to become an expert prospector so that you end up with the nuggets of gold that are buried in your list. The old-time prospectors had a pick, a shovel, a pan and a mule. We have tools too. Postcards, newsletters, Facebook, a blog and transport to visit people.

In the following chapters I am going to help you set up each of those things and show you how to use them. We are then going to look at networking and referrals to make sure that there is always a new seam of gold to mine.

EDDIE AND SANDIE'S STORY

Eddie says "I may be retired and in my seventies, but I still want to be active and earn some extra cash. I used to have a traditional business with premises, expensive vans and staff. At times it was like running a home for the bewildered!

We bumped into our sponsor at various business events and exhibitions. At one of these we had a longer discussion than usual and he showed us the benefits of having a network marketing business.

Our own business was going through a difficult time. We were being squeezed by our suppliers and some of them were "cutting out the middle man" and going direct to our customers. In this horrible situation, I could immediately see the attraction of a business which needed no premises, no staff, no expensive vans and held out the prospect of a residual income which would take care of Sandie and myself as the years advanced.

Of course we joined and the rest, as they say, is history. We have built up a nice little team with members stretching from Yorkshire down to the South coast.

We both love socialising and we gather customers via networking events, referrals and by taking a stand at local events.

These days though we have taken a bit of a back seat as the team drives forward. We are always there with help, advice and support and I can do as much or as little as I like, depending on my energy.

Whatever happens the residual income keeps coming in and that means that we have more options than most retirees. It is a great feeling to get paid over and over again for work we did just once many years ago.

Our distributors and customers are just like an extended family and we love them all".

CHAPTER TWELVE

POSTCARDS

It makes sense to start with those who are likely to be our best prospects. Those are the people with the most ticks against their names. How you do this will depend on how much time you have available to see people but I would suggest that 10 people on your list per week is a good number for this process.

You are going to send "Business Launch" postcards and there are some examples on a following page. You can also download the artwork from the "Smart People Book" Blog. They are my gift to you and you are free to use them in any way that you wish.

Just go to www.smartpeoplebook.co.uk

You can order your cards online from www.vistaprint.co.uk and arrange delivery yourself (by hand or by post).

Or you can use a service which will both print and post the cards for you. You can find such a service here at www.docmail.co.uk

Your third option is to use a local printer. Find out the online cost and armed with that knowledge you can negotiate with a local supplier. There are added benefits of using this option. You will get personal help and advice and because you are giving *them* business they should at least take a look at yours, so you may get a new customer.

On the address side of the postcard you put the recipient's address and a message in your own handwriting which says

"Thought you would like to know"

Sign it and only include your phone number if they are unlikely to know it. Under no circumstances include your website address!

If you use this approach with everyone on your list, you will be putting yourself in a fantastic position.

Take a moment now to imagine that you have just received a very nice postcard from a relative or friend saying that they have started a new business but without any further information. Wouldn't you be burning with curiosity? "I wonder what they are doing?" "I wonder why they are doing that?" Do you think that you might ring them up and ask what it is all about? I can assure you that many people do.

In any event, when you next bump into your friend wouldn't you ask "What is this new business you have started?" or "How is that new business of yours going?" Of course you would.

In one easy manoeuvre, you have achieved what many people find impossible. You have got your friends and acquaintances approaching you and asking you about your business!

You will respond by saying something like this: "I've been meaning to talk to you about it because I think that there may be some benefits in it for you. I can't promise anything, of course, but when can we get together for a coffee (or a beer) (or a glass of wine) and I'll tell you all about it."

Your company or team will have training on what to say at that meeting and how to continue if you can't meet in person. Well done! You have cleared the first hurdle and you are on your way.

But we aren't finished yet. In the next chapter, you will learn all about the newsletter.

VAL'S STORY

I had my own motor racing business from 1979 to 1995 and subsequently worked for a local engineering firm for twelve years. That ended with a "compromise agreement" and the realisation that I didn't want to work for an employer ever again. At the age of 62 I felt too young to retire and, if I did, I would only have the state pension to live on.
I had some fleeting experience with network marketing companies in the past but my experiences hadn't been great and I told myself that I would never get involved again. As it turns out that would have been a very big mistake. It was just a matter of finding the right business for me.

I was approached by people from the same company four times between 1998 and 2007 and refused every time. It just goes to show that timing is everything. In 2008 when my circumstances changed, I decided to give it a go. I contacted the last person who had spoken to me and, much to my husband's annoyance, I signed up. As an aside, my husband has since seen sense and joined me in the business!

Initially all I wanted to do was to double my state pension – so no big ambition. I have easily achieved this many times over and as I got more passionate about the business I realised that I could qualify for all sorts of other benefits. I now have shares in the business (it is a FTSE 250 Company), I have been on three all-expenses paid luxury holidays and qualified for a new car and had the loan of a company Porsche.

Even though I had a motor racing business I had never learned to drive myself so, thanks to the company personal development program and the fact that they gave me a new car, I learned to drive at the age of 65!!

My business has given me many things. I have made lots of new friends and really enjoy helping my team to follow in my footsteps and achieve their goals and dreams. It keeps me focussed and keeps me young. What more could anyone want?

CHAPTER THIRTEEN

THE NEWSLETTER

You are in business and your newsletter is going to help you to stay in business. Don't worry about the technicalities; we will deal with those later. It won't cost you anything except some time and the benefits are huge.

1) You will raise your credibility with everyone on your list.
2) You will have a way of staying in touch with people who are not ready to become your customer right now.
3) You will have a way of staying in touch with those who might join your team but the timing isn't right for them at the moment.

4) You will make all the people on your list even more curious about what you are doing.
5) You can show your team that you are a leader they can respect by giving them access to your newsletter system. You can even let them copy your newsletter if they are uncertain about writing the newsletter themselves.

Are you ready to begin? With each person on your list you are going to approach them with a simple text message. It says this.

> Hi (NAME)
>
> You probably know that I have started a part-time business working from home. It is going really well and I have decided to start a monthly email newsletter. Is it OK to add you to my mailing list?

The response to this message is invariably positive. When they say "Yes OK" send them a second text which says "Which is the best email address for you?"

Make a note of their response and thank them. Do you think they will be curious? Do you think they will bring up your business when you next meet? You bet they will.

Before all this happens, you have to set up your newsletter of course. For this we are going to use an online service called Mailchimp. You can find it at www.mailchimp.com

Using their "Free Forever" service you can have up to 2,000 subscribers and send up to 12,000 newsletters per month. That is way more than you will ever need. Each newsletter will contain an unobtrusive Mailchimp logo which links back to their service but that is a small price to pay for such an excellent system.

So, go ahead and sign up for their free service. It is quite straightforward and you will soon be getting a welcome message from the quirky Mailchimp chimp.

You can download a template for your newsletter at the blog for this book. Just go to www.smartpeoplebook.co.uk and sign up. It is entirely free for you to use and you can share it with your team by sending them to the site so that they can download it themselves.

If you don't like my template then you can use one of those provided by Mailchimp or you can, of course, design your own.

Next you will write your first newsletter. Sending the newsletter to your list is called a "Campaign" in Mailchimp jargon but you will soon get the hang of it.

Your first newsletter is also the most important one that you will ever send. It will get the most "opens" because it is new and people will be curious.

The newsletter should contain your picture and <u>the first section should be about why you have decided to start a part-time business from home.</u> Don't make it too long otherwise people won't read it.

The rest of the newsletter can contain anything you like but make it upbeat and positive. If you have been on training say how much you enjoyed it. If you are getting lots of support from your team say that. If you have attended a team social and met lots of fantastic positive people say that. BUT WHATEVER YOU DO, DON'T SAY ANYTHING ABOUT YOUR ACTUAL BUSINESS AND DO NOT INCLUDE ANY WEBSITE LINKS!!!

I know this may seem strange but, believe me, it is for your own good. You are creating curiosity and you want your friends to burn with desire to find out what you are doing. Nothing good can come from telling them in the newsletter exactly what you are up to.

Let me ask you a question. What would you do if one of your friends had started in a business which you didn't know anything about? If they put the name of the business in their newsletter you would be straight onto Google wouldn't you?

The curiosity factor would be gone. Worse still, they may land on one of your colleague's websites, think it was a good idea and sign up to be a customer or distributor. Only they wouldn't be *your* customer or distributor, would they?

End your newsletter with a joke. Years of experience have taught me that if you want your newsletter to be opened and read on a regular basis you need a "hook" to encourage people to open it. The promise of a joke that they haven't heard before is a very good hook.

Here is a template for the first paragraph of your first newsletter:

Intro for Newsletter 1 (Modify with your own details)

Hi

Thanks for agreeing to go on my mailing list. I hope you enjoy the newsletters and perhaps learn something new. At least I hope you like the jokes!

As you know I have been a shop fitter for many years, but I just couldn't face doing the same thing for the next twenty years until I retired at 65. Who says that you have to wait until 65 to retire anyway? That is why I decided to take action and start my own business working from home part-time. Hopefully the extra income will grow so that after a few years I will have choices which I don't have now.

I am working with a great team and my own personal mentor is helping me learn everything I need to know in order to be successful. I will keep you updated on my progress. Hope to see you soon.

Warm regards

Eddie

[It is important that the newsletter doesn't contain any mention of the company name or any website links. It is designed to build credibility and curiosity with people on your list who are not yet customers]

But what if you don't feel confident about writing the rest of the newsletter or are struggling to find an appropriate joke. Don't worry, I have got your back. Go to the website for this book at www.smartpeoplebook.co.uk and you will be able to download 12 newsletters. That is a whole year's worth of content which you can just modify with your own details.

A competent copywriter would charge you anything up to £100 for a single bespoke newsletter so these newsletters are easily worth £1,000. They are my gift to you for buying this book. To access them you will need to know the password. Please don't share it with other people. The password is "smartpeoplebook2016" (without the quotation marks).

Send the first newsletter to yourself so that you can check that it looks OK and that you have a copy. I will explain why you need a copy in a moment.

Now make your first list by adding all those people who have agreed to receive your newsletter. Give this list a simple name like "Eddie's Newsletter List".

Send newsletter number one to your list; next month send newsletter number two and so on. Just personalise each of the newsletters from two onwards with a short introductory paragraph like "It has been a great month. My business is growing steadily and I have 6 new regular customers. I'm going to a leadership training provided by my company next week – I really can't wait. Hope you are having a great time too and really enjoy this newsletter."

Remember that you kept a copy of newsletter number one? Each time that you add someone to your mailing list you send them this copy directly. It means that they don't have to wait a month before they get a copy and they will be more likely to open it because they only just agreed to go on your list. That is working smart.

Enjoy the newsletters, but we are not finished yet in creating our campaign to build your business. In the next chapter, we are going to look at establishing a social media presence which will attract people to you, help you to support your team and keep you in touch with customers. This is the wonderful world of Facebook.

RUSS & JUDITH'S STORY

Many years ago I was at a networking meeting and was given a referral to Russ and Judith who became customers of mine for the one service that my company was offering at the time. They had a young family. Russ was working at Weetabix and Judith was happily working in the NHS. We stayed in touch and, over time, they added on new services as the company made them available.

In 2009 their circumstances changed and, amongst other things, Russ was made redundant. On one of my regular visits we chatted about joining my business and I left them a DVD to watch. A few days later they joined and we have been business partners ever since. I will let Judith take up the story.

"We joined Eddie's business because the timing was right and we really liked the idea of a residual income that kept on growing. Russ was looking for something different and after 21 years in the NHS I wanted to reduce my hours and have more time to enjoy life.

We love travelling and the income from our business has helped us to have more holidays and to go further afield. Without a boss to worry about we can go whenever we want. This year we have had short trips and much longer ones. Along with other places we have visited Portugal, France and Mexico, sometimes on our own and often with friends.

The business has provided a car, a growing residual income, share options, travel, recognition, training and support.

For many people being made redundant is the start of a downward financial spiral, but in our case it was the springboard to a new life where we are in control of our own destiny. We have built up a wonderful team who are not only business partners but also friends. Recently we have even started to invest in property.

Our growing network marketing business has given us choices and we look forward to many more years of looking after our customers and growing our team."

CHAPTER FOURTEEN

SOCIAL MEDIA

"I don't trust anyone who is not on Facebook.
I think they have got something to hide."
My daughter Claire.

To those of us in the older generation who grew up in a world without social media the above quotation may come as something of a shock, but it is indicative of how the younger generation are thinking. If we are going to have customers or distributors in our team who are not "Old Fogies" we need to have a social media presence.

For a network marketer, Facebook is truly our friend.

We need a Facebook profile which will attract people to us.

We need a Facebook group for our team and we need a Facebook group for our customers.

If you are not already on Facebook, then you need to open an account quickly. It is simple and free. Just go to www.facebook.com

If you are unsure about what to do there is plenty of help online but I am guessing that most of my readers will have a Facebook presence already.

If you met someone socially and wanted to find out more about them wouldn't you check out their social media? Most people would. I am only talking about Facebook, but if you are in business there is a similar platform for business people called LinkedIn. You might want to have a presence there too.

Here is a secret which many people will not tell you. Getting someone's Facebook details and making them a 'friend' is more valuable than getting their phone number or email address. People move and change their address. They may change their mobile phone numbers and they may change their email address but their Facebook account stays the same. You will always have a way to contact them.

On top of that you will be able to see what is going on in their lives. You will be able to be a real friend as they deal with the ups and downs of daily living.

And you will be able to spot when the time is right to talk to them about your products, services or business.

If I went to your Facebook page right now would I see a picture of your face? Would I see pictures of you drunk? Would I see you scantily dressed or in suggestive poses? It is time to clean up your page and make yourself attractive to those who are checking you out. Especially those who are thinking of joining your team.

If you have already started a network marketing business, you may have already formed some social media bad habits.

Let us go through the steps required to bring your personal Facebook profile up to scratch.

1) Your profile picture should be a recognisable picture of you alone. It does not need to be a professional portrait but you should be smiling and people need to be able to tell that it is you. So, no cartoons, no group photos, no pictures of pets, no logos.
2) The header photo or banner should be a picture which shows your lifestyle and definitely not your company. It can be a holiday scene, your family, a sporting scene

and so on. Generally, you want to portray yourself having fun.

3) The "About" section should first include a website. Either a blog or a "capture" page but not your company's website. If you don't have a blog already there is a future chapter with simple instructions on how to set one up.
4) Next your business title. Do not include anything about your business. A simple designation to use is your surname and add the word 'Marketing'. So, if your name is 'Robinson', you would style yourself as "Founder of Robinson Marketing" or "Owner of Robinson Marketing". If you have a partner in the business, you could say "Founding Partner of Robinson Marketing". As an aside, it is useful to have a business name like this for your bank account and for dealing with the tax authorities.
5) Your biography section should give people a little glimpse of who you are and what you do. For example, "I am a family man who decided to start my own business to supplement my income in retirement. I help people to lose weight and increase their fitness level. Many people say that they are healthier and happier than they have been for

many years. I started part-time by fitting my business into the 'nooks and crannies' of the day but after only three years I was able to leave my boring desk job and do this full time. Now my greatest joy is to help others follow in my footsteps. I have a great team who, with my help, are developing their own plan to escape the drudgery of a 9 – 5 existence."

6) Your contact information must include an email address. After all, you do want people to be able to contact you. In the website chapter, we will talk about domain names but an ideal email address would be 'your first name' @ 'your surname'. co.uk or .com. For me that would be eddie@rodwell.co.uk It is easy for people to remember that email address if they know your name.
7) You should include your blog and/or capture page
8) Your phone number is optional. However, it is more business like to include it.

Now, go through your photos and albums and take out any pictures which do not show you in a good light. We all have them and we may have thought them funny at the time, but now we are running a business and we need to be more professional.

Having sorted out our profile and images we now need to start using Facebook in a constructive manner. That means posting every day and more than once a day.

That may seem like a tall order but it only takes a few minutes and is an important part of building your business.

WHAT TO POST

The majority of what you post (say 90%) should say nothing about your business. You can post inspirational quotes and I will show you how to do those later in this chapter.

Short posts should be about life experiences like finding a great recipe, going to a fantastic film or taking a walk in a beautiful location. You could also include a snippet from a motivational book you are reading or a line from a song which means something to you. Holiday photos and photos having fun with your family can also be added.

Another good idea are useful tips. Let us say you had a broken zip and found a video on YouTube which showed you how to fix it. Broken zips are a fairly common problem so you could share your solution and a link to the video.

You might have bought a new pet so add a photo or your old dog may have learned a new trick and perhaps you have a video of him doing it.

Whatever you do, try to include as many images as possible.

You might include a quote from your blog with a link so that people who are interested can read the full article.

You can also include quotes and links to other people's blogs.

The other 10% of your posts should be business related. This could be photos of you with your team either socialising or at company events but NO COMPANY BRANDING! Remember curiosity is your greatest ally and you want to encourage people to ask you what you are doing.

If it is immediately obvious from your Facebook page what your business is about, you will have wasted all your efforts.

It is OK to include educational posts which are relevant to what you do. For instance, if your company has a product which helps people to lose weight you might want to include healthy recipes or nutritional advice.

If your business provides mobile phones you might want to include tips on what to do if you lose your phone or apps you find useful or how to protect your mobile data from hackers.

In a nutshell "Relevant and useful content." You are building up a picture of a happy, confident, friendly expert! Someone people could trust and enjoy being around. If you are not that person already then work on your personal development because it is definitely the person you need to be.

People's Facebook posts tell you what is happening in their lives and there will be times when most people would welcome the business opportunity you are able to offer. Spotting those life situations is relatively easy and will allow you to approach people when they are most receptive to talking to you. The table on the next two pages are a summary of situations to look for. It was first articulated by Andy Waring and it is reproduced here with his permission. Obviously, you probably won't know the situation for sure but you can have a very good guess.

1. Yummy Mummy	20-30+ 2 Kids. Left work to have children but household needs extra income
2. Jaded Executive	40+ Not getting promoted. Stuck in a rut. Scared of redundancy
3. Proto Pensioner	50+ Inadequate provision for retirement.
4. Reluctant Retiree	50+ Made redundant. Can't get another job. Likes to say "I retired early".
5. Ambitious Graduate	Can't get a job. Maybe works in low paid job (McDonalds?) "for CV".
6. Financial Zombie	Heavily in debt. Can meet payments but not paying off debt. If interest rates go up they could lose their home. People on interest only mortgages without any way of paying off the capital.
7. Stuck in a Rut	Unhappy on the verge of taking anti-depressants. No vision for a brighter future.
8. Empty Nester	Family have moved out. "Who am I now?"

9. Late Developer	The track they are on will not deliver on their dreams.
10. Small Business Owner.	Hard working but struggling in a self-created 'JOB'. You say "I've got a way that could add thousands to your bottom line. I don't know if it's for you. Would you be interested in finding out about it?
11. Disillusioned Dreamer	Always had dreams but suppressed them and got a "proper" job
12. Entrepreneur	Thinks big. Always on the lookout for new opportunities. You say "I was at a training where people were explaining how to earn a million pounds a year".
13. Squeezed Retiree	Inflation is eating into their pension which is a big problem now that they are on a fixed income. 70 fit and healthy they could live another 25 years.
14. People like you	Your WHY? Your age group. Occupation.

Original idea by Andy Waring and included with permission - www.andywaring.com

INSPIRATIONAL QUOTES

One of the best things you can post on your social media is an inspirational quote with the words on a beautiful picture. There is a right and a wrong way to do this.

The wrong way is to share someone else's post! It may be a great post but it will give a link from your page back to the original poster.

The right way is to create your own message so that if someone shares it, the link will come back to you. Make sense?

Let us say that I want to promote this book by using quotations. We know that people like cats and like to share pictures of cats so I might create posts like those on the next page.

You will see that if anyone shares them they will also be sharing this book's web link.

"Women and cats will do as they please, and men and dogs should relax and get used to the idea."
Robert A. Heinlein
www.smartpeoplebook.co.uk

"What greater gift than the love of a cat."
Charles Dickens
www.smartpeoplebook.co.uk

HOW TO CREATE PICTURE QUOTES

You will be pleased to learn that making these picture quotations is quite simple and can be done with free resources.

So that you can follow along I have created a video on this book's YouTube channel which you can use to teach yourself. Feel free to share it with your team as well.

First a word of warning. Copyright owners do not like you using their photos especially in relation to promoting a business. So, either use photos which you have taken yourself, buy the rights to use a photo (which can be expensive) or use photos which are copyright free.

Do not under any circumstances use a photo which you have just found on Google by googling "cats" or something similar.

Luckily there is a wonderful picture resource at www.pixabay.com where you can obtain photographs which are free to use even for commercial purposes and without attribution. You don't even have to join the website. However, it is free to do so and it makes things easier if you are a member. Just be aware that the first row of pictures are from Shutterstock and you have to pay for those but the rest of the page and site contains free images.

You will then want to edit the photo you have chosen and add the quotation. You can do that at another free site. Just go to www.ipiccy.com and register.

You can find a video all about using these two sites to create amazing photo based quotations here http://bit.ly/smartpeoplebook

In the video I haven't included the idea of putting your website address on the quotation that you produce. I wanted to keep that nugget for people who actually purchased the book and read it. Let's keep it our little secret!

In the next chapter I will explain how to set up your own website and blog.

CHAPTER FIFTEEN

SETTING UP YOUR WEBSITE

If you have never set up a website or blog before it may seem daunting. Of course, there is an easy way to do it. You can pay somebody.

However, for those of us who are a little more adventurous or have limited means, let me reassure you that it is within the skill set of the average person and need not cost a lot of money.

Once again, I am going to provide you with "follow along" videos so that you can do everything at your own pace.

There are many reasons why you should have your own web presence. Let me list a few.

1. It is a way for people to get to know you.

2. You can use it to get people to subscribe to your newsletter so that you can stay in touch with them.
3. You can use it to promote new products and services.
4. You can use it to help build your list.

Remember that I said in an earlier chapter that your list was the most valuable thing you own? If your company went into liquidation, if your team all left and went elsewhere, if legislation meant that your product or service was no longer viable, you still wouldn't be out of business if you had a list of loyal followers.

If you wish to do business internationally, then a website is essential.

"But Eddie," you may say, "my network marketing company provides me with a wonderful, full e-commerce website, why do I need one of my own?" It is a good question. Most companies will provide you with a website and some may even make it a condition that you *don't* have one of your own. Check out the small print of your agreement with them. But most will not object to you having a blog which does not include their copyright material.

Here is why you need your own web presence.

1. You do not own your company's site and it is designed to promote the company not you.
2. It will, most likely, be what is called a "replicated" site. In other words, it is exactly the same site as all the other distributors in your business will have. The only difference being that it has your name and contact details on it.
3. You cannot easily rank such a site in Google and so anyone googling information about your company is very unlikely to land on your site.

As you can see that site is practically worthless as a business building tool. Don't misunderstand me. It is fantastic for giving to people with whom you have already established a strong relationship but it has little worth otherwise.

On the other hand, you own your own blog. You can work on it so that it rises in the search engines. You can change it on a whim and almost instantly if an opportunity arises. You may even become an internet sensation or at least an internet star in your own community.

You can create a following who will buy many things from you not just those sold by your network marketing company. Selling multiple products to the same customer is a great business plan.

Shall we get to work? I will assume that you know nothing about setting up a website. Let's face it we all have to start somewhere and your website starts with the domain name.

A domain name is the name that a person would type into their browser in order to get to your site. So, to get to the site for this book you would type http://www.smartpeoplebook.co.uk

Modern browsers don't require you to type the 'http://' bit and many don't require you to type the 'www' bit either. Some people make the mistake of typing the domain name into the google search bar. This is a big mistake and will not find the proper website if it is a relatively new site which Google hasn't indexed.

You should not try to get too clever with your domain. The very best name for your blog is your own name and you need to get the.co.uk and .com versions if you can. Of course, if you are not in the UK you should get the appropriate country suffix. If you were in Southern Ireland for example that would be i.e. If you have a common name, that may not be available because someone of the same name has already bought it. In this instance, you need to use a "modifier", perhaps your middle name, your initials or something else. You will usually find something available. Let me give you some examples. Suppose your name is Kelly Short and kellyshort.co.uk is already taken. You could try any of these:

- therealkellyshort
- the-real-kelly-short
- thekellyshortblog
- kwshort
- theblogofkellyshort
- thebestkellyshortblog
- bloggingwithkellyshort
- makingmoneywithkellyshort

I'm sure that you get the idea. You can try out your domain ideas and buy them at a domain registrar. You can't permanently buy a domain. You own it for a specified length of time and then must renew ownership. The cost will currently be less than £10 for two year's ownership of a .co.uk domain and you will find discounts all across the internet. The domain registrar which I use is at:

http://www.123-reg.co.uk You can search for your perfect domain on their front page.

Next you will need hosting for your website. Website hosting is the physical server where your website resides. It is not practical to host the website on your own computer so you need a hosting company who will sell you space on their computers. Hosting companies provide all sorts of bells and whistles but you just need something really basic. I use a company called Hostgator which can be found at: http://www.hostgator.com

But if you have used a domain registrar then they will usually also sell web space and you might find it easier to use them for your first website. The first-year charge at 123-reg is currently £2-99 a month + VAT for registering a single domain and hosting your website.

Now we come down to the big question. How do you design and install an easy to use website if you have never done any web design before?

We are going to use WordPress. WordPress is an open source content management system which, with the benefit of templates, can be used to create almost any website your heart desires. It is also a lot easier than you may imagine.

You will be in good company. According to wordpress.com in June 2016, 26% of all websites worldwide are powered by WordPress.

You can, in fact, have a completely free blog hosted at wordpress.com but I wouldn't recommend that route unless you are desperately short of money. The problem is that you will not actually own the site and wordpress.com could close you down on a whim. You would also have to follow any rules they wish to impose.

Far better to be in control of your own destiny. Get set up with your domain and hosting then follow along with the videos provided at the website for this book. You will be up and running in no time.

Now get some business cards printed and let's go to find some customers and distributors who are not already on our list. It is time to go business networking.

SARAH'S STORY

Sarah was a thirty-something single mum when she joined her network marketing company. Here is her story in her own words ....

"In 2010 I had gone through some personal setbacks (too personal to put in a book!) and left my job as a duty manager in a local Co-Op store so that I could have some time to sort myself out.

Being a single mum meant that I still needed to earn money so I did some house cleaning to bring in the pennies. My energy company was giving me a hard time and my employer referred me to a friend of hers who had recently started helping people to reduce their energy bills.

It turned out that she was working with a network marketing company and she invited me along to a company presentation to find out what the business was all about.

I was immediately hooked by the presentation because I could see how the business worked and how I would finally be recognised and rewarded for the hard work I always put into any job.

One small problem. It cost nearly £200 to join and I definitely didn't have that sort of money. I screwed up all my courage and asked my mother to lend me the money. I really didn't want to do that but it was my only option. Luckily she said "yes" and I was on my way.

Over time I built up a residual income and qualified for a brand-new car under the company's car plan. Unbelievably I also qualified for a 6-star holiday in Las Vegas and was able to take my daughter with me. Everything was paid for by the company. Not bad for a single mum!

Then out of the blue I got seriously ill. I was diagnosed with a brain tumour and needed a major operation. Luckily it proved to be benign but it meant that I wasn't allowed to drive for an entire year. Had I been in any traditional job I would have been in serious financial trouble but the beauty of network marketing, and the residual income it creates, is that the income still comes in whether you are working or not.

The company retrieved my car so I didn't have the worry of insurance and storage and my team rallied around giving me lifts to appointments and training as I recovered.

At the end of that non-driving year I went to the company's head office where they presented me with a brand-new car. Now I am completely recovered and on the road again.

When I first became my own boss in a network marketing business I knew that it was a fantastic opportunity but I didn't see all the benefits that would come my way.

Apart from the holidays, cars and income I have gained something even more precious: I have a new self-confidence and a network of friends who will support me whatever happens. I know that my family's future is secure and getting better all the time."

CHAPTER SIXTEEN

BUSINESS NETWORKING

Business networking events take place all over the world. They usually happen in the early morning or late evening so that they don't interfere with the business day.

They are an opportunity for local businesses to get together, support each other with referrals, exchange local business information and gain useful knowledge. Most of these groups require you to become a member if you plan to go regularly, although they will let you visit a few times without joining so that you can see if their particular group is right for you.

Search Google for "Business Networking" or "Business Breakfast" and you are likely to find many groups in your local area. I belong to two: The "FSB" – Federation of Small Businesses and "BNI" – Business Networking International.

I am a big fan of networking if you run any sort of business and especially if you run a network marketing business. Let me explain why. As a network marketer, you are constantly looking to increase your team. Your best team members will have, or develop, a business attitude which enables them to survive the inevitable ups and downs of life. They will be good at planning their time, have an outgoing personality and realise that success requires hard work and discipline.

An analogy I like to use is this: If your business relied on people being able to swim, which would be your best strategy? Enrol everyone and teach them how to swim or look for swimmers? Both would work, but teaching people to swim would mean your business growing at a much slower pace and many would choose to remain non-swimmers. In your network marketing business, you are looking for people who have a business mentality. Where are you going to find those people? Well, you can teach anybody who joins you or you can go to a business networking meeting and find lots of them who have the necessary skills already.

The vast majority of your business networking colleagues won't be interested in joining your business because they are building a business of their own, but they are entrepreneurs and many entrepreneurs don't like to have all their eggs in one basket. Even if *they* own the basket. In which case, they might like to diversify and add your business to their own. They may also know other people who would be interested in joining your business and they most certainly are likely to become your customers. Especially if you do business with them.

So, if you go business networking you will be "fishing in the right pond". There have been many books written on networking and this chapter can only give you a few pointers. Here are the basics.

- Everyone at a networking meeting is there to promote their own business and sometimes to source suppliers. That means that they are generally not interested in whatever you are offering!
- All things being equal, people will only do business with people that they know, like and trust.
- Business networking is not a quick fix but if you do it properly it will help you to build a

solid network of contacts and that will give you a stable, successful business.

- The meeting is only the start of the process. Your aim should be to meet with people on a one-to-one basis outside the meeting and get to know them better.
- Look for ways that you can help the other members of the group. Can you be their customer? Can you refer other potential customers to them? Do you have a skill or knowledge which would be useful to them? The world loves a cheerful giver and, if you give to the group without any thought of return, you will always have a fruitful meeting.
- Reciprocity works in relationships and in groups. If you give without thought of gain, then in a mysterious way the universe will find a way of rewarding you. I'm sorry if that sounds a bit like something an ageing hippie would say, however, I believe it to be true.

This means you are going to a networking meeting without any thought of personal gain and with the aim of making friends and helping where you can. Still, meetings can be daunting. How exactly do you talk to these strangers and what do you say? The best book I have ever read on this subject is called *Endless*

Referrals by Bob Burg. It is a brilliant read and in it Bob lists ten questions which you can use at any meeting plus one which will set you apart from most other people attending.

With his permission, these questions are reproduced below, but please get his book. It is invaluable.

- How did you get started in the widget business?
- What do you enjoy most about your profession?
- What separates you and your company from the competition?
- What advice would you give to someone just starting out in the widget business?
- What one thing would you do with your business if you knew you could not fail?
- What significant changes have you seen take place in your profession through the years?
- What do you see as the coming trends in the widget business?
- Describe the strangest or funniest incident you've experienced in your business?
- What ways have you found to be the most effective for promoting your business?
- What one sentence would you like people to use in describing the way you do business?

Of course, you need to change these questions so that they suit the way you speak and don't sound formal or forced. You won't use many of them in a single conversation and definitely mustn't use them as a series of quick fire questions as though you were interrogating a suspect!

Perhaps an example will make it clearer. Let's say you have just met Mary, the conversation might go like this.

"Really nice to meet you Mary, what do you do?"

[MARY] "I'm an accountant specialising in helping small businesses reduce their tax liability."

"Wow! That sounds very interesting. How long have you been doing that?"

[MARY] "About twelve years I guess and what do you do?"

"I've just started my own widget business working from home and this is my first networking meeting. To be honest I'm very nervous so I 'm really glad to talk to you because you have put me at ease. You must really love your work if you have been doing it for twelve years. How did you get started?"

[MARY] Well, after I left University I joined a small accountancy practice near where I used to live but then I met John, my husband, and we moved to this area with his employer. I couldn't get an accountancy job with any of the local firms so I decided to give it a go on my own. It was rather forced on me but turned out to be the best thing I have ever done. I found a niche with small businesses and over the years many of them have become my friends as well as my clients."

[YOU] "That sounds fantastic! What do you like best about running your own business?"

[MARY] "I think it is the freedom it gives me. I can choose who I work with and seeing a small business grow and thrive with my help is very rewarding indeed."

Can you see that by using the first two questions you have created a warm conversation and nothing at all seems forced?

Most networking meetings have a structure which means that your conversations tend to be short. If you like Mary and want to add her to your list, you can ask for her card and perhaps suggest that you meet for a coffee at another time so that you can learn more about her and her business. You might even be interested in becoming her client.

Before you part company you may want to use another question from Bob's book which, he says, will set you apart from most other people at the meeting. It goes like this....

"How can I know if someone I'm speaking to is a good prospect for you?"

You already have a list of 200 or more people. There is a very good chance that one or more of those would make a great client for Mary. When you know how to identify a good prospect for her you will be able to go through your list and possibly make an introduction.

Why would you go to that effort? Well there are many reasons.

Mainly you would do it because it is a nice thing to do, but here are some other reasons as well:

1. You will be helping Mary and your friend on the list.
2. It will mean that you and Mary are more likely to become friends and establish a mutually beneficial business relationship.
3. Remember, Mary has a list of 200 too!
4. You will have a happier life. Going about your business making friends and helping people is a great way to live.

Introducing people to prospective clients is known as "Giving a referral" and getting referrals for yourself is the subject of our next chapter.

CHAPTER SEVENTEEN

REFERRALS

Let us make some simple assumptions. You talk to 10 people on your list each and every week. Of those ten, two become customers, one joins your business and the other seven are not interested at all or the timing just isn't right for them. In 20 weeks you will have been through your list and then what do you do?

That is why it is important to continually build your list. Going to networking meetings will help but you need a better way of consistently adding names unless you are going to start advertising. Advertising may be prohibited by your particular company's rules and, even if allowed, it is a quick way to lose lots of money.

A system for gathering referrals is the answer to this dilemma.

If you have a successful network marketing business, you will be providing products or services which are used on a repeat basis. These regular customers can be your source of referrals but you have to have a systematic approach otherwise it will not happen.

Some people seem to have a knack for getting referrals but the majority fail in this regard. They are too shy to ask at the point of sale and then find it difficult to raise the question at subsequent meetings.

At the end of this chapter you will see a referral collection form and you can download the template at the website for this book at www.smartpeoplebook.co.uk

You will use this form in conjunction with "Thank You" cards. My own company supplies "Thank You" cards, but if yours doesn't then you can buy something suitable at one of the card shop chains. I have found them for as little as 10 pence each.

If your company has a referral reward system for your customers (mine does) then make sure that you are familiar with it and how it works. If you don't have that luxury, then work out what five referrals are worth to you and what you can afford to give for receiving them. For most people this is a bottle of wine or a box of chocolates or it may be some free products.

On each customer appointment you go prepared with a pre-addressed Thank-You card and a referral form.

Whatever you are supplying there will be a time lag between the customer ordering and receiving and using the product or service. In my case that could be as much as three months and with some health-related products it may be even longer before the customer really feels the benefits.

We have all had the situation where a sales person had been in our house or office, we have bought something and that was the last we saw of them. No matter how well you know the person you are visiting and how much you might protest that you are not a sales person, I'm sorry to tell you that they will see you as a sales person unless you do something about it.

Your own company will teach you how the sales meeting should be conducted and they may even have training on conducting that meeting with a "canned" presentation. They may also tell you that you are not "selling," you are "sharing". That is just nonsense but used with the best of intentions. Most people do not want to be a sales person as it has become synonymous with "smooth talking" and "sleazy."

If you maintain the charade in your mind that you are not a sales person, then you are unlikely to read any books on selling or take any sales training. That would be a big mistake and you will struggle in your business.

Instead you should decide to become the best, most honest and skilful sales person in your company. That attitude will lead you to unlimited success.

Now I have got that off my chest, and whilst you are coming to terms with being a sales superstar, let us take a look at the sales meeting in someone's home or office.

Firstly, we all know that you are there to discuss business. Even so, you must spend some time building rapport. This means making sure that you are "on the same wavelength" as your prospective customer. Most nice people will offer you a drink. Always accept and if you have a choice I would opt for coffee; people are less likely to ruin a cup of coffee than they are a cup of tea. Also, don't accept alcohol. Making a drink takes time and this is an opportunity for you to build that all important rapport. There are whole books written on the subject but really it is very simple. Be yourself, ask open questions and look for areas where you are similar to your prospect.

Again, this all goes back to when we were cavemen. Your prospect is unconsciously checking you out to see if you are part of the same tribe. In general, we like, feel comfortable and will do business with people who are like us.

Don't move on to the actual presentation until you have established this rapport. Before you do anything else you must set up the opportunity to get referrals. Explain that it is your own business, why you started and the fact that you only work on referral. That part may go like this...

"As you know, your brother Tony recommended that I came to see you because he has been a customer for a few months now and thought that you could benefit too. I started this business because I loved the product myself and wanted a way of earning a little extra money so that my wife could stay at home and take care of our new baby Camilla who is just three months old. I only work on referral so once you are entirely happy I will be asking you to recommend me to other people you know, who could benefit. Is that OK?"

At the end of your presentation they will have become customers and now you are going to set yourself apart from most other people. You let them know that you are coming back!

Psychologically, this does several things in your customer's mind.

It tells them that you are confident in what you are selling and that they will be happy with their purchase. It reassures them that if they have any problems or niggles they will be seeing you again. They know that they will be kept up to date with any new products and will be able to ask any questions about using the product or service which they haven't thought of already. They also know that if you only work by referral lots of other people must be happy clients too.

The referral form has three sections. The first section is the date and time of the meeting when you plan to return. I have found that if you suggest the day of the week and time of the current meeting but at a future date, most people will find this is convenient.

The next section tells your customer what the meeting will cover. You will amend this list to reflect your particular offering.

The third section describes your ideal referral. My business is about helping home owners save money.

You will describe the ideal person for your business. There is space for five referrals. Put your contact details at the bottom and you are done.

I would say something like this. "My ideal referral is a happy smiley person like yourself and your brother Tony. Preferably they will own their own home and have a job which means that they won't have a problem paying our bill! Of course, if they like to save money, I can really help.

I bet that you can think of a few people like that right now. As you think of them just pop their names down here and I will collect the list from you when I come back. My contact details are here at the bottom so if anyone wants to see me before that please just give me a ring."

When you leave your appointment, there is one last thing to do. Remember your Thank-You card? Fill in an appropriate short message and post it. If they became customers it will say "Thank you for becoming a customer and I look forward to seeing you again on ...."

If they didn't become a customer for some reason, you can still say something nice. For example, "Thank you for seeing me this evening. I'm sorry that we couldn't help you due to your current situation but I look forward to helping you at a future time."

What do you do with cards that you receive? It is almost a reflex action for people to put them on display. That means that visitors to the house will see the card and that will give you the opportunity of another referral.

Review and Referral Meeting

Date: ______________________________

Time: ______________________________

AGENDA

1. Review of the Services already supplied
2. Update on Changes and Service improvements
3. Additional services (if required)
4. Review of Bill to make sure savings are maximised
5. Question and answer session
6. Referral List

MY IDEAL REFERRAL

- Happy smiley person ☺
- Home owner
- Employed

- Likes to save money

Who do you know like that?

Name	Relationship	Phone	Address
1			
2			
3			
4			
5			

"Thank you for trusting me with your referrals."

CHAPTER EIGHTEEN

PAST, PRESENT AND FUTURE

We have come a long way, haven't we? From 1897 when my father was born, we have arrived at the present day. Network marketing has been our financial salvation and we are mortgage, debt and worry free. We have a team of thousands of distributors all over the country which means that we could go to the far North of Scotland or the Devon coast and be among friends. Our greatest joy is to head for Europe in our motorhome and know that our income won't be affected. We have toured Italy and Ireland, visited the Vatican and Venice and met many wonderful people along the way.

In this book, I have tried to give you an insight into what it takes to build a business. I have given you my own tools, in the book and online, to enable you to follow in our footsteps. The rest is up to you.

Let me finish by telling you about Cubic Zirconia.

Cubic Zirconia is a manufactured substitute for diamonds. It is very cheap. A diamond which might cost £1,000 could be simulated by a Cubic Zirconia gem costing less than £1.00.

An experienced jeweller can tell them apart but it is very difficult to do so by sight alone. You need to test them. Cubic Zirconia is heavier than an equivalent diamond. A diamond generally has flaws whilst the zirconia is flawless. A diamond is harder than the *fake* but to determine that you may have to damage the gem.

What has that to do with us?

It happens to be a very good analogy when applied to looking for distributors to join our team. We all like to think that we can pick out the *real gem.* The truth is that we can't. What looks like the perfect flawless distributor may well turn out to be too soft and not the real thing after all. The only way to know for sure is to test them.

Everyone that you know, everyone on your list, deserves to be given the opportunity. If anyone could tell, just by looking, who would make a really good distributor that person would become wealthy beyond their wildest dreams. You may even be a real gem yourself and not know it! The only way to determine the truth is by testing.

The real diamond distributor tends to have some common characteristics with the real gem.

- It is very rare for either to be perfect.
- A diamond is formed under pressure and a good distributor is shaped by, but doesn't collapse under, the pressure of the business.
- A diamond sparkles and so do the best distributors.
- Diamonds can be found in jewellery and watches, drill bits and lasers. They can be a thing of beauty or a real workhorse industrial component.
- Distributors can be high flyers in the city, have the most menial of jobs or no job at all. The business will test them.
- The diamonds will show themselves by their sparkle and resilience.

Unlike the gemstone though, we can all *decide* to become a diamond. What we are or what we will become isn't written in the stars. It is a decision.

If you haven't done so already, why not decide that you are going to be a diamond? A person who, despite a few flaws, everyone acknowledges is a real gem! Hopefully, someday soon, I will be sitting in the audience watching you sparkle and shine on stage at your company event.

I look forward hearing about your success. Why not share your progress on the book's Facebook page at www.facebook.com/smartpeoplebook ?

SUGGESTED READING:

The Power Of Positive Thinking – Norman Vincent Peale

Endless Referrals – Bob Burg

Go Pro – Eric Worre

79 Network Marketing Tips – Wes Linden

Success: The Glenn Bland Method – Glenn Bland

Questions Are The Answers – Allan Pease

The Slight Edge – Jeff Olson

Start With Why – Simon Sinek

Winning With People – John C Maxwell

How To Win Friends And Influence People – Dale Carnegie

The Four Color Personalities For MLM – Tom 'Big Al' Schreiter

Unlimited Power – Anthony Robbins

Rich Dad Poor Dad - - Robert Kiyosaki

The E-Myth Revisited – Michael Gerber

Building Your Network Marketing Business – Jim Rohn (Audio Only)

There is a specialist bookseller called "Knowledge Is King" who supply books which are of interest to people involved in Direct Sales and Network Marketing. I really encourage you to join their "Book of The Month Club".

www.knowledgeisking.co.uk

Contact me:

If you have questions or would like more information about working with me and perhaps joining my team, you can contact me by email at eddie@smartpeoplebook.co.uk

Alternatively, use the contact form at www.smartpeoplebook.co.uk

If you would like a phone call then please include your mobile number and a 'best time to call'.